owya

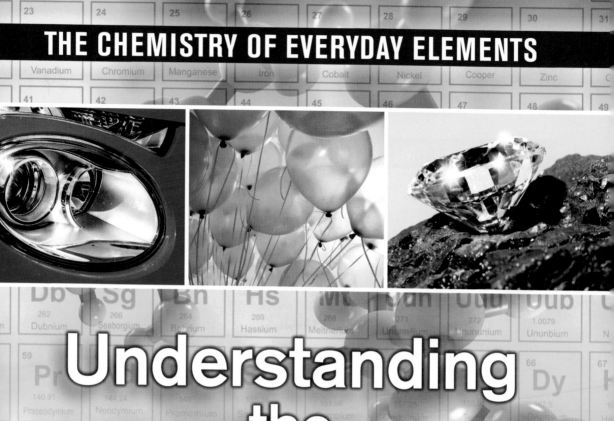

THE CHEMISTRY OF EVERYDAY ELEMENTS

Understanding the Periodic Table

MC

Mason Crest

THE CHEMISTRY OF EVERYDAY ELEMENTS

Understanding the Periodic Table

By Jane P. Gardner

Mason Crest

450 Parkway Drive, Suite D

Broomall, PA 19008

www.masoncrest.com

Series ISBN: 978-1-4222-3837-0
Hardback ISBN: 978-1-4222-3846-2
EBook ISBN: 978-1-4222-7951-9

First printing
1 3 5 7 9 8 6 4 2

Produced by Shoreline Publishing Group LLC
Santa Barbara, California
Editorial Director: James Buckley Jr.
Designer: Patty Kelley
www.shorelinepublishing.com

Library of Congress Cataloging-in-Publication Data on file with the Publisher.

Cover photographs by Dreamstime.com: Sebastian Kaulitzki (bkgd); Pawel Opaska (tl); Konstantin Sutyagin (tc); Richard Thomas (tr); Antonio Guillem (bl); Infocus (bc). Department of Defense (br).

QR Codes disclaimer:

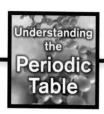

Understanding the Periodic Table

KEY ICONS TO LOOK FOR

Words to Understand: These words with their easy-to-understand definitions will increase the reader's understanding of the text, while building vocabulary skills.

Sidebars: This boxed material within the main text allows readers to build knowledge, gain insights, explore possibilities, and broaden their perspectives by weaving together additional information to provide realistic and holistic perspectives.

Educational Videos: Readers can view videos by scanning our QR codes, providing them with additional educational content to supplement the text. Examples include news coverage, moments in history, speeches, iconic moments, and much more!

Text-Dependent Questions: These questions send the reader back to the text for more careful attention to the evidence presented here.

Research Projects: Readers are pointed toward areas of further inquiry connected to each chapter. Suggestions are provided for projects that encourage deeper research and analysis.

Series Glossary of Key Terms: This back-of-the-book glossary contains terminology used throughout this series. Words found here increase the reader's ability to read and comprehend higher-level books and articles in this field.

Introduction

Can you put the world in a chart? On the Periodic Table of the Elements, you will find information about all natural, and artificially made, elements on Earth and in the universe. Everything you see around you, everything you eat or breathe, everything in outer space, and even the very cells that make up your body is made of elements.

The chart takes its name from the "periods" into which it is arranged. The general properties and characteristics of the elements, repeated in a pattern, let scientists (and students) focus their learning, rather than memorize all 118 elements.

This book will explore the periodic table. Learn how it was developed and about the scientists who contributed to it. Find out how to use the table, and what all those numbers and letters mean. Read about some of the controversy surrounding the discovery and naming of the elements on the table. Not only is it a tool, but the periodic table tells quite a story as well.

Periodic Table

The Periodic Table of the Elements is arranged in numerical order. The number of each element is determined by the number of protons in its nucleus. The horizontal rows are called periods. The number of the elements increases across a period, from left to right. The vertical columns are called groups. Groups of elements share similar characteristics. The colors, which can vary depending on the way the creators design their version of the chart, also create related collections of elements, such as noble gases, metals, or nonmetals, among others.

Understanding the Periodic Table

WORDS TO UNDERSTAND

atomic number   the number of protons in the nucleus of an atom

atomic weight   also atomic mass; the total of the number of protons and neutrons in an atom

density   relationship of the mass of an object relative to its volume

element   pure substance with only one type of matter, which can't be broken down by chemical methods

nomenclature   a shared system of naming similar things

History of the Periodic Table

Open the front cover of any chemistry textbook and there it is: the Periodic Table of Elements. It includes all the elements known to humankind arranged in numerical order from 1 to 118. **Elements** have been known to science for much longer than the table has existed. To help understand the elements and how they worked together, the table was created as a guide understandable across the barriers of language and time. Many, many scientists contributed to the arrangement of the elements in this chart, but it was a long process.

When only a few elements were identified, it was more of a challenge to arrange them in some meaningful way. For example, in 1750, there were only 16 elements that had been

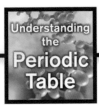

Lavoisier is sometimes called the father of modern chemistry.

discovered and whose properties had been explored. One of the first attempts to arrange the known elements into some sort of pattern was in 1789, when Antoine Lavoisier, a French chemist, classified the known elements as gases, metals, nonmetals, or earths.

Others continued the attempt to organize. For example, in 1829, Johann Döbereiner found groups of three elements with similar properties. He pointed to the fact that lithium, sodium, and potassium shared chemical properties. These three elements are all metals, they have similar melting and boiling points, and are nearly the same **density**.

A Key Meeting

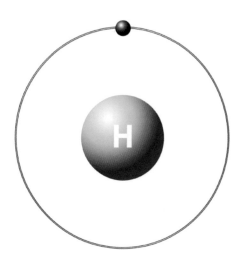

Hydrogen, with one electron (red), is the simplest of the elements.

These were all important advancements and scientific thoughts, but the real work on organizing the elements in a meaningful way didn't take off until 1860. In May of that year, scientists around Europe proposed the idea of the first international conference of chemistry. The chemists wanted to gather to collaborate on issues such as the **atomic weight** of elements, chemical notation, and **nomenclature** standards. The meeting was held from September 3–5 in Karlsruhe, Germany. Not all of the issues were resolved, and disagreement still surrounded the concepts of atomic and molecular weight. However, one of the settled issues was that of the concept of the atomic weights. Before the meeting, there were different ways to talk about the atomic weight of an element. At the end of this meeting, the scientists were in agreement to accept a value of 1 for the atomic weight of hydrogen, an atomic weight of 12 for carbon, and

oxygen (note: later corrected to 8). This gave chemists a standardized starting point for the description of all other elements known at the time. The scientific community looked at the conference as a starting point for a real attempt to organize the elements in a meaningful way.

One Author, Many Helpers

Traditionally, Russian scientist Dmitri Mendeleev is given credit for developing the periodic table in 1869. While his contributions were truly groundbreaking and helped shape the world of modern chemistry, there also were other scientists who made contributions along the way.

One was Alexandre-Emile Beguyer de Chancourtois. He was a geology professor from France who helped with the classification of the elements as much as some other early scientists. He used the atomic weights of the elements to arrange them in a unique pattern. He published his arrangement in 1862. He devised what became known as the "telluric screw," a three-dimensional arrangement of the elements. He arranged the elements in a continuous spiral around a metal cylinder. The cylinder was divided into 16 different parts; 16 because oxygen was given the atomic weight of 16 and all other elements were compared to it. All the elements known at the time were plotted, by their atomic weight, on the cylinder. When the metal cylinder was rotated once, certain elements that shared physical and chemical properties, arranged themselves into a vertical line. Every 16 positions on the cylinder showed the same (or similar) properties. There were problems with this arrangement. Not all the properties or similarities between elements were correct or accounted for. But this was the first time that there was an arrangement of the elements based on their atomic weights. The idea that elements with similar properties can be arranged in a systematic order was a significant contribution to science.

British chemist John Newlands

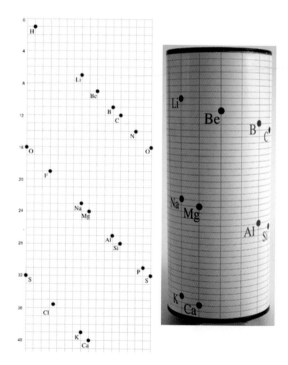

Chancourtois's telluric screw can be made on a paper roll, too.

began to notice patterns among the known elements. Working in the mid-1860s, he noticed that elements with atomic weights that differed by seven shared some similar properties. He called his findings The Law of Octaves, comparing it to the octaves of music. Newlands arranged the elements into a table as well. He sometimes had to put two elements into one box to keep with the pattern he devised. He also had no gaps in his table, something that later arrangements had.

When Mendeleev published his table of elements in 1869, Newlands claimed that his was the first table of elements to be developed. The Chemical Society was not willing to support his claim, and his accomplishment was not credited. In 1998, the Chemical Society, under its new name The Royal Society of Chemistry, erected a plaque in Newlands' honor in London that reads "J.A.R. Newlands 1837–1898. Chemist and discoverer of the Period Law for the chemical elements was born and raised here."

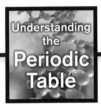

Newlands was honored by the Royal Society of Chemistry.

In the years between 1864 and 1870, German chemist Julius Lothar Meyer developed several different tables to arrange the known elements. The first table he developed had 28 elements. He arranged them according to how many other elements they

Meet the periodic table!

could combine with. He expanded upon this design and in 1868 published a table that included more elements, arranged in the order of atomic weight. However, he was unable to publish his work until 1870, a year after Mendeleev's periodic table. While his might not have been the first table published, Meyer made other significant contributions to the arrangement of the elements. He is credited with being the first scientist to notice the periodic trends in the elements.

More About Mendeleev

Mendeleev is credited with developing the table of elements upon which our modern day periodic table is based. He developed his table while trying to organize the elements in 1869. He wrote the properties

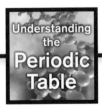
of the known elements on cards and began arranging them. He found, after many, many tries, that when he put the element cards in order of increasing atomic weight, certain patterns began to appear.

His arrangement not only worked for the elements that were known, but it worked for undiscovered elements as well. Mendeleev left gaps in his table for elements whose properties he predicted but that had yet to be discovered. In the first two decades after his table was published, several elements were discovered that

Dmitri Mendeleev made key advances in organizing the table.

showed his predictions to be correct. Mendeleev predicted that an element, which he called eka-aluminum (the element after aluminum), would have an atomic weight of about 68. In 1886, the ele-ment gallium was discov-

Gallium has a very low melting point and can turn to liquid when held in the palm of a hand.

ered that had an atomic weight of 69.72 and the same properties that Mendeleev had predicted.

There was a point in time when it looked as if perhaps Mende-leev's table had some serious flaws with its organization. In the 1890s, Britain's Sir William Ramsay discovered the noble gases (for which he later won a Nobel Prize). These did not seem to fit into Mendeleev's table; in fact they seemed to actually contradict his arrangement. That is, until Mendeleev realized that these gases fit into a final column on his table, which gave the table batches of eight related elements rather than of seven, as Newlands had discovered.

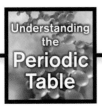

One More Twist

There was still one last twist to the arrangement of the elements that needed to be determined. Mendeleev arranged his elements by atomic mass. And, in most cases, this is the same order as the **atomic number** of the elements. But there were exceptions, such as iodine and tellurium.

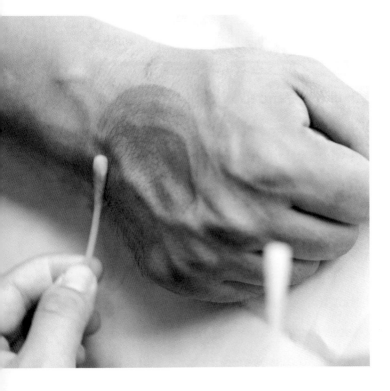

When Mendeleev was arranging the elements, he found that some elements were in what he would consider to be the wrong place based on their atomic weight. Iodine and tellurium were two such elements. If the elements

The element iodine is often used in medicine to disinfect skin or wounds.

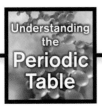

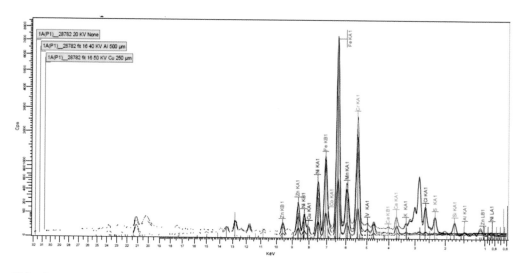

This chart shows the results of X-ray examination of a sample of elements.

were in the wrong place, he would move them to where he thought they should be. Originally, he had iodine and tellurium in their correct locations according to atomic weight, but when he discovered that iodine had properties similar to the halogens and that tellurium was similar to oxygen and sulfur, he switched their locations. He was unable to explain these discrepancies.

English scientist Henry Moseley came up with the answer. He used X-rays to measure the wavelengths of the X-rays given off by the elements. Using this information, he was able to mathematically measure the atomic number of the elements and find their proper place in the table. Unfortunately, Moseley was killed by a sniper in World War I

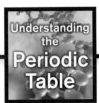

and was not able to finish his work, but others have carried on, finding other new ways to measure elements.

The work of filling in the table continues, with new elements being discovered and their place being chosen on the table. Read Chapter 4 to find out more about those pioneering efforts.

Henry Moseley's contributions were cut short by his death in World War I.

Text-Dependent Questions

1. Name two scientists besides Dmitry Mendeleev who contributed information to the forming of the periodic table.

2. What is the atomic weight of carbon?

3. From what country was Mendeleev?

Research Project

Read more about Dmitri Mendeleev, especially the story of how a dream helped him come up with his periodic table. Write a short report with more specifics of how he put together the basics of the table we use today.

Understanding the **Periodic Table**

WORDS TO UNDERSTAND

atomic mass unit (amu)   the smallest unit used to describe the mass of atoms; 1 amu = 1/12 the mass of a carbon atom

reactive   in chemistry, able to change or connect with other substances

representative elements   elements in the first two columns of the periodic table

A Tour of the Table

The modern periodic table, the one found in the front of a chemistry textbook or on a T-shirt in a novelty store, is an arrangement of squares into horizontal rows and vertical columns. The table gives useful information about each element as well as general information about trends and properties among similar elements. Let's take a closer look at the different parts of the periodic table and the properties that are found there.

Square Up

Each element occupies its own unique square on the periodic table. If you compare different copies of the periodic table, you'll probably find a slight difference in the information

in each square. Some include the element's name, while others may include an indication of the structure of the electron. But nearly all representations show the following three things: the unique chemical symbol of the element, the atomic number, and the atomic mass. For example, the box representing the element zinc may look like the photo to the left:

This indicates that the unique chemical symbol for zinc is Zn. Zinc has the atomic number 30, and it has an atomic mass of 65.38.

Chemical Symbols

Each element has a unique chemical symbol. This may be a one-, two-, or three-letter symbol. Elements such as oxygen, hydrogen, carbon, and nitrogen are all represented by one letter, written as a capital letter. Oxygen is O, hydrogen is H, carbon is C, and nitrogen is N. These are fairly easy to remember—they are the first letter of the element's name.

The majority of the elements are represented by two letters, with the first one capitalized and the second lowercase. For example, neon's chemical symbol is Ne, and zinc is Zn. Other elements do not have chemical symbols that are as easy to interpret. Tin, for

Atoms

An atom is the smallest particle of an element that still has the chemical identity of that particular element. Atoms are made up of three different types of particles: protons, neutrons, and electrons. Protons and neutrons are found in the center of an atom in an area called the nucleus. Electrons spin around the nucleus at varying distances from the center. Protons have a positive charge, neutrons have no charge—they are neutral. Electrons have a negative charge. Another way to look at the atom is as a positively charged central core surrounded by a negatively charged "cloud."

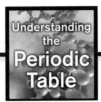

Titanium takes it name from the Titans, a group of Greek gods.

example, has the chemical symbol Sn, while lead is Pb. Gold and silver have the chemical symbols Au and Ag, respectively. As you will read in Chapter 4 of this book, many elements have names based on Greek or Latin words, or characters in mythology, or even the name of the scientist who discovered them.

A few elements have three letters in their chemical symbol. The first letter is capitalized, while the other two are lower case. Uuo (ununoctium) and Uup (unumpentium) are two examples. These names are in the process of being officially named so they may not appear in that manner on all copies of the Periodic Table.

Atomic Number and Mass

The atomic number of an atom of a particular element is equal to the number of protons in the nucleus. Every element has its own unique atomic number. When looking at the periodic table, you will notice that nitrogen (N) has an atomic number of seven. This means there are seven protons in the nucleus of the nitrogen atom. No other element has seven protons in the nucleus. Hydrogen has only one

Xenon in its gas form is often used inside the vacuum glass surrounding car headlights. The gas provides a very clear medium for the light to shine through.

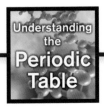

proton in its nucleus, while xenon has 54.

The mass of an individual atom of an element is measured in **atomic mass units**, or **amu**. Protons and neutrons in the nucleus have approximately the same mass. (The

The Elements Song

mass of an electron is much, much smaller.) Therefore the atomic mass of an element is equal to the number of protons plus the number of neutrons in the nucleus.

A close look at the square for boron on the periodic table shows that boron (B) has an atomic number of five and an atomic mass of 11. There are, therefore, five protons and six neutrons in the nucleus of an atom of boron.

Rows and Columns

The periodic table is arranged in rows and columns. Each of the horizontal rows is called a period. There are seven periods on the table. The first period has only two elements—hydrogen and helium. Periods

2 and 3 each have eight elements and periods 4 and 5 each have 18. Notice how periods 6 and 7 have a group of elements below the main table that are extensions of the period. There are a total of 32 elements in each of those periods. This is the current arrangement of the 118 known elements. As new elements are discovered, this might change.

Certain properties of elements change as the elements range from left to right across the rows of the periodic table. For example, the size of an atom generally decreases from left to right within a period.

Read from left to right across the periodic table, as the atomic numbers increase.

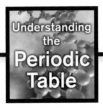
The horizontal columns on the periodic table are also called groups or families. These represent elements that have similar properties. At the top of each column is the group number. Depending upon which particular design of the periodic table is used, this may be written in one of two ways. In many cases, the **representative elements** are given group numbers with an A after it. The transition elements, which are located in the lower sections of the table, have a number followed by the letter B. Other tables number the groups in order from 1–18.

Silver and gold are the most famous of the transitional metals.

Meet the Groups

Some of the groups of the periodic table have names. Group 1A elements are known as alkali metals. These are shiny

Fluorine

Fluorine is one of the most **reactive** elements on the periodic table. It's a very corrosive and toxic gas. If fluorine is

stored or used for experiments in a glass container, it will react with the glass to form a new substance. Fluorine must therefore be handled in containers made of Teflon or copper to prevent this from happening. This gas is also used safely in toothpastes, mouthwashes, and other oral products in the form of fluoride.

and soft metals. These elements, including lithium, sodium, and potassium, conduct electricity and heat. They also react with water and if combined with oxygen, will form a white substance. Alkali metals are so soft that they can all be easily cut with a knife. The shiny new surface that is exposed after it is cut soon tarnishes in the air. In fact, these elements need to be stored in oil so they do not tarnish. Alkali metals have a variety of applications in the real world. Rubidium and

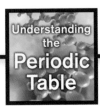
cesium are used in atomic clocks to keep very accurate time. Sodium is used in high-intensity lamps and is one of the two elements found in table salt.

The Group 2A elements are also called the alkaline earth metals. These are also shiny metals. However, they do not react as readily

Thank the element strontium for being part of the mix that makes red fireworks.

with other elements, especially when compared to the alkali metals. These elements do occur naturally in nature, but they usually are not found alone—they are combined with other elements. There are many uses of the alkaline earth metals as well. Calcium is an ingredient in building materials. A compound that contains strontium gives some fireworks a red color. Radium is a radioactive alkaline earth metal. In the past it was used to make paints that glowed, and was added to drinking water and toothpaste before the dangers of radioactivity were understood.

Group 7A is known as the halogens. The term halogen means "salt-producing." Halogens, if they react with metals (especially the group 2A alkaline earth metals) will form salt. Halogens are very reactive. As a result, these elements can be very harmful, and even lethal, to living things.

The Group 8A elements, or noble gases, are very stable elements. The noble gases do not readily react with other elements. These elements were actually discovered by accident. Scientists were looking at the properties of nitrogen and discovered that the density of nitrogen they made in the lab was different from the density of nitrogen in the

air. They realized that there must be something in the air that actually hadn't been discovered yet. What they found were the noble gases.

Metals vs. Nonmetals

You'll find aluminum to the left of the zigzag line that divides metals from nonmetals.

There is one other significant feature on the periodic table. Many versions of the table have a zigzagging line from boron down to astatine. This line, generally speaking, separates the metals from the nonmetals. With the exception of hydrogen, the elements to the left of the line are metals, and those to the right are nonmetals.

Metals are shiny elements that are solid at room temperature. They are ductile, meaning they can be drawn into a thin wire. They are also malleable, which means they can be pounded into a thin, flat sheet. Metals are all

Mercury is a metal, but melts very easily. It's often used in thermometers.

good conductors of heat and electricity and melt at high temperatures. (There is one metal that is not a metal at room temperature. Mercury, with the chemical symbol Hg, is a liquid at room temperature. Mercury is used in thermometers, dental fillings, and in fluorescent lamps. Mercury is very toxic and when it builds up in the body's tissues can damage the brain, kidneys, and lungs.)

Nonmetals are not usually shiny in appearance. They don't conduct electricity well, and can't be hammered into thin sheets or drawn into a wire.

Finally, the nine elements located adjacent to the thick zigzag line are called metalloids. Locate boron, silicon, germanium, arsenic, antimony, tellurium, and polonium on the periodic table. These elements

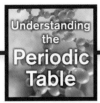

Silicon's ability to conduct electricity very well, while maintaining a lightweight yet strong form, makes it a key part of photovoltaic solar cells.

exhibit some properties of metals and some properties of nonmetals. They are, for example, better conductors of electricity and heat than nonmetals are, but not as good as metals. Metalloids are called semiconductors. This means they can be altered to function as either a conductor or an insulator. Because of these properties, silicon is a metalloid used, in electronics and in solar panels.

Wherever they are located on the periodic table, by row or column, in one group or another, every element is vital to life on Earth.

 Text-Dependent Questions

1. What is the chemical symbol for zinc?

2. What is a noble gas?

3. What does an element's atomic number represent?

Research Project

Pick your favorite element from the chart. Do some research and find 10 ways that this element is used in the world, from everyday life to scientific research, in products that we use, or in experiments for discovery. Make a poster about what you discover about "your" element.

WORDS TO UNDERSTAND

geochemistry   the study of the chemistry of the
rocks and minerals found on Earth

hydrocarbon   an organic compound that contains
only hydrogen and carbon

ion   an atom having an electric charge because of
the loss or gain of electrons

Using the Periodic Table

The Periodic Table of the Elements is a tool. It is used by chemists, geologists, biologists, and students everywhere. Understanding the patterns and the relationships on the periodic table is very useful—it prevents us from having to memorize it! Let's take a quick look at some of the many ways that scientists and others use the periodic table.

Chemists

It's not surprising that chemists—scientists who focus on the study of matter—use the periodic table. All matter is made up of elements, and the periodic table unlocks information about physical and chemical properties of all the elements.

A familiar sight? Students in chemistry classes often study how elements interact with one another in chemical reactions.

Remember that one of the pieces of information found on the periodic table is the atomic mass of an element. A chemist may want to determine how many atoms of sodium are in a one-kilogram block of sodium. This can be done using the periodic table.

Chemists are very concerned with chemical reactions. Chemical reactions are processes in which one substance (or several substances) is changed into another substance or substances. In order for this to happen, the bonds that hold atoms together must be broken. The bonds of the individual atoms themselves are not broken, so it is possible to look at the elements on the periodic table both before and after the reaction and understand their properties. Chemists are often particularly concerned with the concentration of the elements in the reaction, as this determines how fast the reaction will occur. They use the periodic table to calculate those concentrations. Molecular weight is the sum of the atomic masses of all the elements in a molecule. The periodic table is an invaluable tool for this sort of calculation. For example, a molecule of water has two atoms of hydrogen and one atom of oxygen. A quick glance at the table shows that an atom of hydrogen has an atomic mass of 1.00794 amu and the atomic mass of one atom of oxygen is 15.9994. So, when added up, water's two hydrogen atoms and one oxygen atom have a total (rounded) weight of 18.01. This may not seem like a significant bit of information to everyone, but this is big stuff to chemists and can help shape their understanding of a chemical reaction.

Other scientists may be looking to conduct scientific experiments. Before mixing chemicals, it is important to have an understanding of what might happen. While they may not be able to accurately predict the exact changes that will occur, a look at the periodic table and the properties of different elements may prevent an unfavorable reaction. For example, mixing alkali metals, such as sodium or potassium, with water could create a flammable gas!

Biologists

Biologists study life and the processes that help living things survive. Their focus in chemistry is around the elements that make up organisms. They study organic chemistry—which is the chemistry of organic compounds. Organic compounds are any compounds containing carbon and hydrogen. They may also have other nonmetals in their structure, including oxygen, sulfur, nitrogen, or phosphorus. Organic compounds are everywhere. Commonly known as **hydrocarbons**, these molecules make up things like gasoline, medicine, plastics, and most of the food we eat.

Geologists

Geologists study Earth and the processes that shape its surface. Geologists need to use chemistry and therefore rely on the periodic table for much of their work. Some geologists are concerned with minerals and their composition. Minerals are naturally occurring compounds. These compounds are made of elements and get their properties from the elements that make them up. Mineralogists, as well as other geologists, are concerned with the melting point of minerals or the temperatures at which they become solid as they form from cooling magma or lava. This is information that can be found by studying the properties of the elements on the periodic table.

Geochemists look at how geology and chemistry are related. Sometimes, they may look at the specific ways that a rock or mineral can be dissolved by water. Or they may look at how a rock will change over time as it is subjected to heat and pressure. These are all properties that are based on the elements that make up those rocks, and that information comes from the periodic table.

Scientist vs. Scientist

Scientists of different scientific disciplines use the periodic table, but those who aren't chemists sometimes

A geologist would look at the periodic table in a different way than a chemist would.

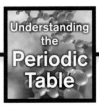
complain about the structure of the table. For example, some biologists have reworked the current periodic table a bit to focus on the elements that are most important in the study of life. This includes an indication of how abundant each element is in the human body (if at all), and information about the roles of trace elements, micronutrients, and other elements in our cells. The idea is to create a more "biology-friendly" display of the elements while still emphasizing that the need to understand chemistry is inherent in many different sciences.

It's a bit more crowded (and looks better online), but this is an Earth Scientist's Periodic Table, reflecting the needs of that brance of science.

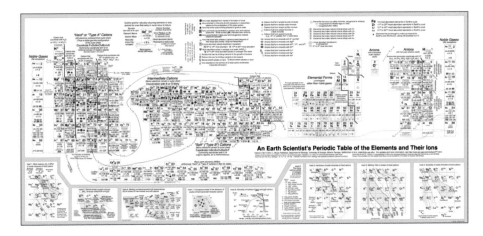

There has also been a version of the periodic table adapted to earth scientists and geologists. This table highlights trends that are important in **geochemistry** and mineralogy. This version of the table arranges the elements by their electrical charge,

Organic compounds

rather than by their atomic weight. This distinction is important in geology because the minerals that make up the Earth's crust are made of elements with electrical charges called **ions**. The elements on the periodic table do not have a charge. The properties of minerals, such as how easily they dissolve or the temperature at which they melt, all depend on the size, structure, and charge of an ion. Arranging the elements in an order that is based on those properties makes it easier and quicker for geologists, and students of geology, to use the information.

The General Public

The periodic table serves as a scientific tool, but many consider it to be rather artsy as well. You can purchase colored copies of the

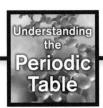
periodic table in the form of posters, place mats, and T-shirts. Books have been written highlighting each of the individual elements on the table, with pictures and photographs of each element. Coffee mugs and mouse pads can be found in the offices of teachers, scientists, and science fans alike. The idea of the table has also been used to

 Periodic Table Humor

Believe it or not, people have made up jokes based on the period table. Many of the jokes use the chemical symbol for an element, so it really pays to know the chemical symbols!

• Do I know any jokes about sodium? *Na*

• Are you made up of Copper and Tellurium? *Because you're Cu Te.*

• I heard oxygen and magnesium just broke up and I was like O Mg!

"organize" all sorts of non-chemical information, including superhero powers, sports cars, and presidents. How do you proudly announce to the world your understanding of the elements?

 Text-Dependent Questions

1. What is the molecular weight of water?

2. Name a science other than chemistry that often uses the periodic table.

3. What information do geologists wish was in the classic periodic table?

Research Project

Go online and find an artist who has used parts of the periodic table in his or her creations. Using those as examples, make your own piece of art using all or part of the table.

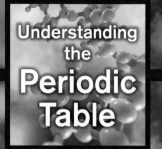

Understanding the Periodic Table

WORDS TO UNDERSTAND

half-life the amount of time it takes for exactly one half of a radioactive element to decay, or break down into another substance (plural, half-lives)

radioactive decay the process by which an unstable nucleus of an atom breaks down, resulting in the release of energy

synthetic not naturally occurring, made by humans

Discovering New Elements

As of early 2017, there were 118 known elements on the periodic table and, thus, in the universe. Elements with numbers 1 to 92, with two exceptions, are found naturally on Earth. Some of them are very abundant, while others are only found in very small amounts. The other elements, numbers 93 to 118, are **synthetic** elements. They are only made artificially in a laboratory, often existing for a tiny fraction of time. These elements are known as the transuranium elements, because they come after element 92, uranium. It is quite possible that these elements were found on the planet early in Earth's history. They may have broken down through the process of **radioactive decay** into lighter, more stable elements.

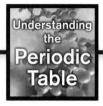
The two elements that are not found naturally on Earth are technetium (Tc) and promethium (Pm). Technetium, atomic number 43, is very unstable. Any Tc that was on Earth when it formed nearly 4.6 billion years ago has decayed into other elements by now. Tc has been located in some stars in the universe. Promethium is also unstable and its isotopes have very short **half-lives**. It has also been observed in some stars and is in trace amounts in ores of uranium here on Earth. But because it is so unstable, even the Pm that is in those ores never accumulates to a significant level.

"Making" New Elements

Today, the synthetic transuranium elements are produced in the lab in two different ways: neutron bombardment and fusion. During neutron bombardment, elements are made to absorb more neutrons. Remember, this does not change the atomic number of an element, but it does change the atomic mass. If this heavier isotope of the element is unstable, it may break down. Sometimes when this happens, a neutron is changed into a proton, thereby changing the atomic number and thus revealing a new element.

The First

Scientists at the University of California at Berkeley (right) created the first synthetic element using a particle accelerator to collide the atoms at speeds about one-tenth the speed of light. The result was element number 93, called neptunium, after the planet Neptune. In 1941, scientists bombarded uranium with hydrogen and got the element plutonium (number 94). Plutonium was found to decay spontaneously, and release a tremendous amount of energy in the process. Several years later, plutonium was used in the atomic bomb dropped by American forces over Nagasaki in Japan near the end of World War II.

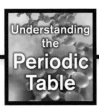

The other way to make a new element is by the process of fusion. Fusion is the process by which lighter elements are joined together to make heavier elements. Both of these processes are complicated and sophisticated. It takes years to produce new elements, and sometimes all the hard work just doesn't pay off.

This press conference in Moscow celebrated a new element named for the city.

Now that 118 elements have been identified, manufactured, and named, what is next? Thanks to Mendeleev's periodic table, it is possible to predict the properties of elements even before they are found. It is even possible to predict where on the periodic table they would fit. For example, element number 125 has not been discovered or manufactured in a laboratory yet, but when it is discovered, it will be at the start of a new row of transition metals.

Scientists aren't exactly sure how many elements they will be able to make in the lab. Or how many others they will discover naturally. Some think that there is an infinite number of elements that could be made, but others are not so convinced. They think that eventually the elements would become too heavy and would instantly break down, as they would be very unstable. In fact, some of the most recently discovered elements existed for tiny fractions of a second. No matter how many are discovered in the future, the process will be very long and arduous since it is becoming more and more difficult to manufacture the heavier elements.

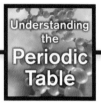

Naming Elements

The elements on the periodic table got their names from a variety of sources. Some were named using ancient languages, others after a place, and still others after people. Elements like gold, iron, and copper got their names from Anglo-Saxon languages. Often, Latin names come through in the chemical symbol of the element. For example, the Latin word for gold is *aurum*, which is why gold has the chemical symbol Au. The Latin word for iron is *ferrum*, explaining the symbol Fe to represent iron.

It was a common practice for elements to be named for places, usually the place where the element was first discovered, or manufactured. For example, Europium (Eu) was named after the

A plaque in Ytterby, Sweden, notes it as the site of major element discoveries.

continent of Europe. Americium, francium, and polonium were named after the countries they were discovered in. Californium (Cf) was first manufactured in a lab in 1950 at the University of California at Berkeley.

Announcing new elements

One village in Sweden, called Ytterby, was where four different elements were discovered. As a result, ytterbium, yttrium, erbium, and terbium were all named in Ytterby's honor. Only one known element was found in space before it was found on Earth. That is the element helium, named for Helios, the Greek god of the Sun.

Other elements are named after mythical creatures or stories. Tantalum (Ta, atomic number 73) is a rare, bluish-gray metal named after the villain Tantalus from Greek mythology. Titanium also gets its name from Greek mythology. The element was named in 1795 by its discoverer, German scientist Martin Heinrich Klaproth, after the Titans of Greek mythology. In 1949, scientists manufactured promethium in a laboratory. It was not an easy process to make this new el-

ement. Therefore they named it after Prometheus, the character from Greek mythology who was sentenced to a life of torture and sacrifice for stealing fire from the gods.

Other elements are named after the scientists who discovered them. Usually, this is an honor given to the scientist after they have died. For example, curium was named after the Curies, and einsteinium after Albert Einstein. The only time that an element was named after a living scientist was when seaborgium was named after Glenn Seaborg, a chemist at UC Berkeley.

Since 1947, the International Union of Pure and Applied Chemistry (IUPAC) has been the organization tasked with approving the names of all newly discovered elements, and determining the symbol by which the element will be known as on the periodic table. The naming process begins with the scientists who discover the element. They are asked to propose a name, and a symbol, for the element. The IUPAC also recommends that any new elements end in "-ium" for continuity with the current elemental names.

Controversy in Chemistry

Despite all the regulations surrounding the naming of elements, conflicts arise. The controversy surrounding elements 104 to 109 resulted in a nearly 40-year long debate. The problem surrounded the practice of letting the element be named by the person, or people, who discovered them. With elements 104 to 109, laboratories in different countries were working to manufacture these elements in their labs. The properties had already been predicted and the race was to

Scientist Ernest Rutherford was honored by having an element named for him.

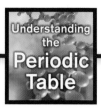
be the first to successfully manufacture them. In this case, it wasn't a matter of "discovering" the element, but a case of "making them first." Several groups all claimed to have discovered the same elements at roughly the same times. The right to name the elements was not clear. For example, the American team wanted to name element 104 rutherfordium, after Ernest Rutherford, known as the father of nuclear physics for his contribution to the understanding of radioactivity. A Russian group claimed to have discovered the element first and therefore reserved the right to name it kurchatovium, after Igor Kurchatov, a Soviet nuclear physicist. Similar debates raged over elements 105 to 109. Finally in 1997, the IUPAC General Assembly met in Switzerland and assigned the following names to those elements:

- 104 rutherfordium (Rf)
- 105 dubnium (Db)
- 106 seaborgium (Sg)
- 107 bohrium (Bh)
- 108 hassium (Hs)
- 109 meitnerium (Mt)

California's Lawrence Livermore Lab gave its name to element 116.

The Newest Elements

Surprisingly, the elements aren't always discovered in numerical order. Recall that the properties of the elements, even the undiscovered ones, have been predicted for a long time. The discovery of the elements, or the production of the elements in most recent cases, has more to do with the capacity and success of lab work than anything else.

For example, the last five elements to be discovered were elements 114 to 118. Elements 114 (flerovium) and 116 (livermorium) were discovered by a group of Russian scientists in 2004. Element 118 followed in 2006. Finally, in 2010, elements 115 and 117 were discovered. These elements were not named, or even announced to the public, at the time of their discovery. The discovery has to be con-

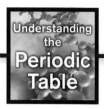
firmed, and replicated, by at least two different labs before the IUPAC even will consider adding it to the periodic table.

The year 2016 was an important one for the periodic table. The following elements were finally given proposed names. Here is a summary of their names and the reasons behind their names:

Japanese scientists discovered and helped name element 113, nihonium.

- **113 Nihonium (Nh)** This element was the first element to be discovered in Asia. The name comes from the word *Nihon*, a name for Japan that means "Land of the Rising Sun."
- **115 Moscovium (Mc)** This element was discovered in a lab in Moscow, Russia.
- **117 Tennessine (Ts)** Researchers in Tennessee,

at Oak Ridge National Laboratory, Vanderbilt University, and the University of Tennessee at Knoxville, worked to discover this element.

- **118 Oganesson (Og)** This element was named for Yuri Oganessian, a scientist who worked on super-heavy elements.

These elements filled in the seventh row on the Periodic Table. Unless any of the names are disputed, they will join the others on every Periodic Table of the Elements, covering classroom walls and textbooks pages around the world.

 Text-Dependent Questions

1. What was the only element named for a living scientist?

2. What was the first synthetic element?

3. True or false: All the new elements discovered are very stable.

Research Project

Using elements not listed in this chapter, find the background or naming reason for five other elements.

FIND OUT MORE

Books

Dingle, Adrian, Simon Basher, and Dan Green. *The Complete Periodic Table: All the Elements With Style!* London: Basher Science, 2015.

Gray, Theodore. *Elements: A Visual Exploration of Every Known Atom in the Universe.* New York, NY. Black Dog & Leventhal, 2009.

Wiker, Benjamin D. *The Mystery of the Periodic Table.* Bathgate, ND: Bethlehem Books, 2003.

Web Sites

www.webelements.com/
One of the most visited and informative websites about the elements of the periodic table can be found at this link:

www.ptable.com/
Interact with the periodic table here at this website.

iupac.org/
Curious about all things related to chemistry? Take a look at the official website for the International Union of Pure and Applied Chemistry. It sets the standards for naming new elements!

SERIES GLOSSARY OF KEY TERMS

carbohydrates a group of organic compounds including sugars, starches, and fiber

conductivity the ability of a substance for heat or electricity to pass through it

inert unable to bond with other matter

ion an atom with an electrical charge due to the loss or gain of an electron

isotope an atom of a specific element that has a different number of neutrons; it has the same atomic number but a different mass

nuclear fission process by which a nucleus is split into smaller parts, releasing massive amounts of energy

nuclear fusion process by which two atomic nuclei combine to form a heavier element while releasing energy

organic compound a chemical compound in which one or more atoms of carbon are linked to atoms of other elements (most commonly hydrogen, oxygen, or nitrogen)

spectrum the range of electromagnetic radiation with respect to its wavelength or frequency; can sometimes be observed by characteristic colors or light

solubility the ability of a substance to dissolve in a liquid

Understanding the Periodic Table

INDEX

Photo Credits

About the Author

Jane P. Gardner has written more than 30 books for young and young-adult readers on science and other nonfiction topics. She authored the *Science 24/7* series as well as several titles in the *Black Achievements in Science* series. In addition to her writing career, she also has years of classroom teaching experience. Jane taught middle school and high school science and currently teaches chemistry at North Shore Community College in Massachusetts. She lives in eastern Massachusetts with her husband and two sons.